# GONE
# GONE

TODD MEYERS

# GONE GONE

Duke University Press
*Durham & London* 2025

PROJECT EDITOR: LIVIA TENZER
DESIGNED BY COURTNEY LEIGH RICHARDSON
AND TYPESET IN GARAMOND PREMIER PRO
BY COPPERLINE BOOK SERVICES

Library of Congress Cataloging-in-Publication Data
Names: Meyers, Todd, author.
Title: Gone gone / Todd Meyers.
Description: Durham : Duke University Press, 2025.
Identifiers: LCCN 2024024171 (print)
LCCN 2024024172 (ebook)
ISBN 9781478031642 (paperback)
ISBN 9781478028451 (hardcover)
ISBN 9781478060666 (ebook)
Subjects: LCSH: Drugs—Overdose—Poetry. | Drug abusers—
Family relationships—Poetry. | Grief—Poetry. | LCGFT: Prose
poems. | Experimental poetry.
Classification: LCC PS3613.Y4774 G66 2025 (print) |
LCC PS3613.Y4774 (ebook) | DDC 811/.6—dc23/eng/20241105
LC record available at https://lccn.loc.gov/2024024171
LC ebook record available at https://lccn.loc.gov/2024024172

Cover art: Wolfgang Tillmans, *last still-life, NY,* 1995.
Courtesy of David Zwirner, New York; Galerie Buchholz;
and Maureen Paley, London.

for Stefanos

# CONTENTS

This book represents an attempt to write through the grief that follows overdose death and what surrounds it. If it has any purpose, it adds a tiny but dense counterweight to writing that places the political economy of addiction ahead of the veracity of loss. It is essay and ethnography, conjured and churned. I have no easy answer for what to do with the disturbances that encounters with others produce. I committed to my notes a record of certain moments—moments in the moment or moments immediately following words spoken and observations made. But I am left wondering why the light of these encounters enjoys more attention than the shadows they throw. I took touch and with it kneaded in the dreamlife that comes after. The field and its record-as-ethnography occupy that place where the nightmare and the feelings it stirs in the first moments of waking are indistinguishable.

I defend the necessity of contact and the mess it creates. I can never escape the need of ethnography, the more-ness it promises and abuses. I believe the ethnographer is an important instrument of contact and interpretation, but somewhere along the way this instrument has been assigned a single task, namely the collection of words. Words fail grief not because they are unable to hold the experience, but because when received they are assumed whole and unbroken, not as words as much as captured facts. —and writing grief, reduced to reporting these facts with a puzzling mix of neutrality and inscrutability, does not acknowledge, as Denise Riley writes, this "altered condition of life."[1] I care about something stirred in encounters, a record that calls on the same intensities the sayer invites the hearer to join. I am guided by a hope that by joining I might give expression to a form of living that sheds light on what that form does and denies.

What follows is not one story but many. You might ask, and rightly so, *What is there left to say?*—or better, *What is there left to know?* I was cautioned early in my inquiry that grieving of this kind was always more or less the same. I was told that what distinguishes this form of grief from others is the intensity of regret, unease, and shame that characterizes it. I thought, *What loss doesn't already traffic in such worry?* But I underestimated what it takes to offer even a hint of how unwieldy this grief can be for those who remain.

I agree there is something particular here, something about drugs and dependency and the weight they carry, or rather the weight they require others to carry. There is also something hard and necessary about positioning oneself along the breakwater between the flattening totality of addiction and harm, and the love and rage that sit on the other side of grief. I may know loss, but I also know that this gives me little clairvoyance or access to the wild and inventive shape it takes in other lives. The swirl of grief that surrounds fatal overdose invites understanding as a ruse; it twists efforts to find relief. Not once but again and again, tirelessly, unforgivingly.

But I continue to stick my nose into lives and deaths that are not my own and tell myself that what I am seeking is one story with many voices. In the pages that follow, each story is carried by the same three names, each committed at once to their differences and likenesses. In this way I do not challenge this grief's special character, nor do I attempt to correct the misattribution of sameness, nor do I seek to put on display the assortment of experiences that surround this all too ordinary form of death. If all stories share a common thread, so be it. I allow myself to be taken in by the claim that every word drifts to a single point. I let the slippage between the singular and the plural test that claim. I give the whole endeavor over to those individuals generous enough to talk with me about loss, again and again, layer by layer, together.

—always together.

NOTE

1. Denise Riley, *Time Lived, Without Its Flow* (London: Picador, 2019), 13.

# I.

## ALL IS ALL NOW

All is all that's left.                     nothing has been emptied.
when it starts to leak, something immediately tops it   off.
replenished.               incessantly.     predictably.
with other things. always other things to disguise absence.

"Imagine worrying's end," Ely says.     —to be released from
sleepless nights. Texts, phone calls, a fist hammering the
front door at odd hours. Imagine the guilt that flows from
relief. Maybe not *from* but *alongside*.

    waters merging.

    Marie-Ève has been gone for two years.

The paths siblings travel sometimes diverge, imperceptibly, often coldly, eventually. —misunderstandings or exhaustion, dull bickering and a latent acrimony too easily stoked.  distances grow. These are the something-nothings of relatedness, a thousand strings that crisscross between those who share genes. But some things are not-nothings, some things cause the relationship between a brother and a sister to swerve wildly, unexpectedly, pulling one onto the path of the other. Ely traded resentment for a dimensionless kindness the first time Marie-Ève overdosed.

—she fell, he would catch her.

next time.

Already by age eleven there is no story of him that isn't also a story of her. He gave love, unconditionally, and that love was returned to him, undiminished.

Dusk, out with his friends on bicycles, racing home as streetlights blink to life, already late, passing frenzied through sheets of cool, moist evening air, invisible and dense.

—racing, bursting and breathless. His sister giving cover when his mother's scolding begins— *où étais-tu?!* —hand raised.

She received him when no one else did.

Her scent floating across the dinner table.    cigarettes and the flat, choking-flowery sweetness of whatever perfume she used to unsuccessfully cover up her smoking. Fingernail polish remover and Mountain Breeze fabric softener in lieu of cleanliness. *Beautiful.* It was the assimilation of odors he would forever associate with teenage girls, taken from this moment and others. *Beauty.*

—the shape of his future longings.

—and awe, his, in the face of anyone who came even remotely close to her, to Marie-Ève.

few did.

When Ely's sister found herself on a different path, he followed, not happily but willingly. She needed him. He received her when no one else did. The two years that separated them meant nothing. Her little brother big-brothered her. But now, to overtake her in years. her age forever fixed at the moment when she disappeared from his life. he never sought to outgrow her.

Marie-Ève stayed on his couch.

Mornings: prework ritual coffee and cigarettes. Catherine, Ely's *blonde*, sat with Marie-Ève by the open window, washed in the spring sun's soft angles, warm and pollen dusty, the aroma of night lingering in musty corners and dying shadows.

The 1990s Québec ska hit "Tassez-vous de d'là" ("Get out of the way") by their favorite band, *Les Colocs*, played

they sang along

all three, pitifully, unapologetically nostalgic.

—a friend in bad shape, cocaine eyes and heroin blood (*Y'avait d'la coke dins yeux, Y'avait d'l'héro dans l'sang*), but on the part of the singer crushing cowardice in the face of his friend's need: I am the coward of cowards (*Je suis le lâche des lâches*) / What do you do in times like these (*Qu'est-ce qu'on fait dans ce temps là*) / Me, I just want to run away (*Moi j'avais l'goût d'm'enfuir*) / I left him alone on the edge of catastrophe (*Je l'ai laissé tout seul au bord de la catastrophe*) / Forgive me, forgive me (*Pardonne-moé, pardonne-moé*)—

Marie-Ève's occasional girlfriend would arrive just in time to kill the mood and they would all leave for work.

Her first overdose wasn't even a party. He repeats the phrase she used to remind himself of her surprise and

sorry.

not even a party.

It took her girlfriend two days to call, two days before Ely was aware that Marie-Ève had nearly died. It was not uncommon for her to disappear for a few days without notice. He had mixed feelings about an empty couch. He was also undecided about the times she occupied it.    keeping his eye on her was not what he wanted, ever.    her life, not his.

All the resentment he might have felt for Marie-Ève was gladly placed on her girlfriend. Stupid. Arrogant. Danger-o-fucking-boy-unbelievable.    —who does that? — who keeps a person      in the dark           for two days?

She returned and placed herself under a kind of house arrest. Ely was fine with that.      her life, not his.

It lasted one week.

He tells me that she does not belong to these
moments. He is telling me about her, in the moments that
led up to her death, not because he wants to, or even
because she would want him to, but because talking about
what comes next is the assignment he's been given. *I know,
I know, there's more, tell me more, name everything
different, anything different.*   *yes, go on*     I recognize
the imposition, my imposition, the narrowness and forced
self-consciousness that acts as a form of     re-death-ing.
a death of the parts that have nothing and everything to do
with this last moment, her last moments, before all these
other, realer moments fade.

what of what comes between?

but we are somehow compelled to measure significance by
absence.

editing a life.   whittled down to disappearance.

He clung to her, attached himself to her with his
worry.    slippery    and she and his worry colluded against
him, they exchanged masks, took on the same voice, their
differences harder and harder to discern.    but not always.
not after.    it is all too clear now.    the wrong clarity.

a hard clarity.

*Go on.*

Marie-Ève got an infection after letting a friend pierce her belly button. "It was free!" she insisted. Ely reminded her that most infections are. They made fun of her for days. They rolled up their shirts to the midriff in mock solidarity. Ely even dabbed his belly button with Catherine's lipstick and called himself Marie-Ève's infection twin. "But it's cute, right?" She was committed and endearingly vain, which only prolonged their teasing.

In full sun Marie-Ève and Ely decide to walk over the Jacques-Cartier Bridge. both feel in need of exercise. The beers in his rucksack offer a counterweight to piety. Halfway across the St. Lawrence River the bridge drops down to Jean-Drapeau Park on Île Sainte-Hélène. On the far side of the park, they know a place accessible through a slim labyrinth of humid underbrush and weed trees, along a black, soggy path that leads to a small inlet facing the rapids between them and Île Notre-Dame, an artificial island built for the Expo 67 world's fair. the god-like nerve. Their spot is shady and quiet; even the sound of the racing water is muffled by leafy branches of elm hanging like a wave about to break. a few branches touch the water. light moves through the trees, a strobe, cool, and then tiny flashes of yellow heat, embracing, warm, blinding, diamonds.

They once saw a sturgeon here, the long boney ridge and dorsal fin twisting unmistakably on the surface a few yards from where they dangled their feet in the icy water. bait. ancient fish and small glimmers of treasure. —sun on something metallic under the water, reflecting off the inside of a discarded potato chip bag, for a second, bullion, dazzling, a different flash, another

kind of embrace, something like hope, for a second, treasure
hunters. cameras flash at the two lucky lotto winners holding an
oversized novelty cheque, grinning stupidly and truly. the promise
of riches, a hope that gives special incomplete warmth. wonder
and newness.

they look for arrowheads.                        together.

waters merging.

Returning from the river he allows himself to daydream. he
feels a deep urge to lose himself in the wooded marsh they just
passed.         he shares this thought, and she joins in. 48 hours
later a search party is dispatched, thrashing tidy rows of wet tall
grass as it advances, safety-vested and stoic, a slow crooked line of
volunteers and police.         to be lost and found, or.     safe or
not.     to be found, or not. *go on.*

daily she passes the downstairs neighbors, fat shirtless sentinels,
television blaring day and night, the soundtrack accompanies their
stoop-sitting-watching.
*Ne conduis pas gelé!* (Don't drive high!),     grunted, a public
service announcement-cum-insult spit through few teeth.
the older and the younger.     treacle and halitosis.     she
goes out for the evening. One or two long-term tricks have
come home with her, public-private lives on full display,
a sudden license for dick-holding grab-assing judgmental
smirks.         toothless.         men.

Everyone knows where people have died.     a landscape of half-acknowledged memorials. But people also know where everyone got laid or broke up or got in a fight or when her boyfriend called the cops who just laughed at him and told him to start acting like a fucking man, so there's that, too.

Over there lived the guy who was in a band in the early 2000s you wouldn't know if you didn't grow up here,

but we all did.

so, there's that,                                    too.

the guy's sister still lives somewhere around here.

          memorials to the faded.

          Ely's friends from this time are long gone, moved, absorbed into family life, or expelled from it, children and rocky relationships, preoccupied with jobs or not having one.     His contact with them is broken, their voices and bodies faded, but their absence carries no weight.    none.    it does not form a hollowness.     it is an absence that needs no form and gets none. they are gone, pale but within reach, and with minimal desire or willpower, returned.

          Marie-Ève exceeds his touch.
          there is no reaching,

her.

She is gone gone.

Gone Gone.

What could be more final?

*turn the page.*

Ely's life is measured in broken furniture.

Marie-Ève's life, the tally of shoplifting convictions.

Catherine remembers her clients as good people.          hard,

but good.

They both had standing appointments with Catherine
the first day of each month at the social services center.

If they didn't show up, she would find them later that day with
a group of friends—not-quite-friends, not-quite-fiends—
at a popular hangout by a subway grate near the Préfontaine
metro station. The spot was climate-controlled. trains passed
underground, a rush of cool air through the grates in the summer,
warm air in the winter. Marie-Ève and Ely had used together for
several years, a couple—or not-quite-a-couple, not-quite-not—
maybe "team" is more accurate.

they had been together since 2005.

so much history.

Ely left the foster care system as soon as he could. Marie-Ève could not remember when she left home, but she knew there never existed a time before her desire to leave.

Nothing explained the opposing forces at work in their lives, between order and disorder—their daily undoing, their uncommon discipline to take daily meds for HIV, the need for lab work and visits to the clinic.

Predictability.

Catherine was instrumental, anchoring.    predicable, kind.

Ely zigzags across rue Hochelaga, *à la recherche de* cigarettes at the *depanneur*. Cars avoid him. Ely's shirt hangs out of his back pocket in a game of flag football.
He throws an empty can at one of the cars.

The driver pulls over.

Ely erupts in directionless rage. mass conspiracy,

everyone.

Police arrive.

# Fuck fuck fuck.

# Osti d'crisse de tabarnak!

He left. You say certain forms of absence are not hard to
sense.        they're absences felt more than thought.
or maybe heard, in the fitful silences afforded by absence.


    *certain forms of absence,*        lord-y,


do these things ever announce themselves obliquely.
through habit and certitude, they let the feeler know that
hurt doesn't always require        sentimentality. or
understanding.


Catherine marks all these places, people-places, along the
street. She sees another Ely and another Marie-Ève in the
park near the bike path she uses every day.        another
close-enough, as-themselves-enough but similar-enough,
enough-to-be-legible-to-her in the way Ely and Marie-Ève
were once legible.        among so much illegibility.
she slows        and waves.
neither acknowledges her.


six months is probably enough time to register change.
*right?*
or three months.


or even a few weeks.


but definitely more than a few days.
change comes on all-of-a-sudden and is felt slow.

*and more and more.*     *turn the page.*

it's been three weeks since she has had to find new routines to care for the kids. Marie-Ève tells me she'll get back to me if she has time.

End of the day, dusk.

*honestly.*     *she asks.*     *what did he leave behind?*

# Fentanyl. &
# child support.

# Farewell to chlamydia. & dirty jokes.

so many things disappeared with him.   that she loved.

II.

# AFTER-
NESS

Night is full of missing persons.      it belongs to them.

He woke up, she did not.            neither returns.

     Her purple flesh gentle with pink spider webs blue lips & gray skin. limp. our deaths before NARCAN. not ours, or

     his.

     hers.

     Puce. her sick was puce. he finally remembers the word. her loss expands his color palette.

What is it about the gel orange hum of night streets that lulls
humans into a sense of shelter? the dimly lit in-between spaces
in cahoots with darkness. —we might find a clue in how our
subconscious remembers the color of day passing through
a mother's flesh, brightening the uterine world we all once
inhabited.    alone    each in our dawn orange womb-home, in
suspension. surely there was once or twice in the story of a mother
when her life was lit wildly.    the nocturnal city shares this
unborn orange, dimmed as it passes through folds of protection,
our cocoon, reaching us unexpected and new.

we still crave it, surely,
        enough to put up with all the rest.

Who doesn't smell this orange?
garbage subway air and old grease.                its invitation

and danger?

primitive memory of this first light likely keeps us ignorant
of shadows and what might lurk there. or maybe it is safety
itself we're so eager to reject. the necessary desire to leave
the nest or the cave, to be or become.        warmth and
affection short-circuit our objective need for self-preservation
against a plotting chiaroscuro.

it is this original light that cannot be returned to us,

though we want it.

Catherine's children were taken from her a year before she passed. she died in that moment; all the rest was postscript.

that much was obvious, he says.

We are lucky it rained, it cooled things down a bit. a shower always clears the air, a reboot.

The water doesn't pool on the sidewalks for long. its vapors either return immediately to the heavens or find soft passage downward.

so woefully biblical these moments after a rain.    flood, rebirth.

How deep does it sink, this rain, through the street, asphalt rubble clay and dirt    before it makes its way upward again? there must be a point during its passage when it decides to make the return, when its material and spiritual circumstances cause this sunken rain to reverse course. there must be a moment in its journey when descent becomes ascent.

Oh, to be so lucky.

We dug a hole for our things. Our aim was to smother them, some-other them, some-mother them.    to cover them over, to remove them from our sight, to extinguish remembrance, to un-member them.    we commit burial, to disappear them, to erase them, with no attention to decency.

What we didn't know then was that such an act was only temporary     concealment, a kind of not-quite-entombment in service of a some-day-return.  so woefully, woefully biblical.  our unwitting transaction was to offer these objects to the ground to be transformed. In doing so, we not only transformed them, these objects, but the earth that surrounded them as well.  paper and fibers and small flakes of metal and plastic separated from the soil, sucked out and joined with dirt, broken zippers and torn seams, a hand, kneading these things, doing work unseen.

over time —weeks? —decades? this turning and stretching causes them to become one.
a some-thing-unrecognizable in parts, altered under the soil as one.

and then the rain, passing over these now changed things, things-changed-now one newly-joined-thing, the rain, traveling deeper and deeper into the earth, refuses to take this

only-now-one-thing with it, into the depths,
                    but with the movement of each

drop downward, the rain pushes this thing, whole and changed, upward, aiding its return, to make space for the rain's journey downward in exchange, returning this thing to the surface before the rain's own return, a prelude to its own changed course.

The churning world under our feet, and the objects now
indistinguishable from the medium that holds them,
together urge a return.

          nothing ever stays buried.   not really.
          such a long road to arrive at a simple point.

night's orange un-still. its vibrations pantomime an unseen drama
beneath us, the ground throwing its voice.

there is no center, nothing to offer direction, no horizon to
level us off. our ears refusing to clear as we slowly lose
altitude.   tinnitus ringing, loudly.   heavy.   a blanket over
our senses, no signs to guide us.          dampened, distracted.

                    Night.

      She waited for a   pinch of remembrance, the memory of
him, to visit her in the dark, but it came on slow, the morning after
the endless night.      it was a restless leg.  a surge of intrusive
thoughts.        a sore shoulder.   She would turn over and
over in bed, a nocturnal pro wrestler flip after flip piledriving the
pillows and mattress into submission.

      Remembrance is a body without rest.

it.
it is the hunger for reprieve through distraction, which is
just the fucking worst. really. and it is the worst because it

works—kind of—, but only for a moment.        and even in the
moment of working, it does so just long enough, just enough-
enough to feel the lingering absence of relief.        distraction's
phony efficacy,
        plugging away at its promise and wrongness.

She asks, "Why can't a return be a return?"                we
crave wholeness, and finitude.
we crave the fullness of apparitions and phantasms and
ghosts.        we would even settle for the occasional
poltergeist.        of course, we're all too clever for any of
this. we know this is not a return, not a real one anyway.
ours is a gray mass that rests in the chest. an ache that
burrows into the lining of the stomach, to linger and grow.

                        Night.

        we celebrate broken bits or leftovers because we know
that's all we're going to get.        and all we're ever going to get.
        so, start getting used to it.

        it.

it.
it hates the words of others. it resents sharing its memories with
them.        it burns it down to start again.        it makes closed fist
threats and refuses eye contact.        it doesn't sweat the small stuff,
*barf.*        it still needs to do the dishes, empty the litter box, stop
scrolling on its phone, wipe piss off the toilet seat.

it answers emails and sends fresh "hope this finds you wells."   it
needs a lay and a nap and a marriage of both.
it.
it desires a space for all the things that cannot be said.
the accumulation of things that refuse us.

Streetlights.

Marie-Ève could see from her kitchen window the slow falling
dander of cottonwood trees. Each white-puff feathery seed floating
weightless, producing a different time signature than the world
around it.   bright and perfect.          not snow, volcanic ash.
a freeing catastrophe in slow-mo.          just close your eyes and
let it take you.   gathering in gutters and at the edges of sidewalks
after its soft journey.

She takes stock of her surroundings. The screen on the kitchen
window is torn, bugs are entering and exiting at will. The fruit
fly situation needs to be addressed, and soon. Her refrigerator
is buzzing.          loud. it is crying out for the drawers to be
removed, soaped and scrubbed and returned.          crumbs.
everywhere.   tiny holes in the walls left by the previous
tenants.          she doesn't see them anymore, but she does.
She loved to make her bed as a little girl. she cannot remember the
last time she has even changed the sheets.

There sits a box of his things.   she prays nothing in there
is rotting.          it will live in the hallway.          after him,
untouched.

This is her time of debris. she has lived in ruins without letting
them in.        now is her time to feel ruins.



Night.

If you travel between the railway tracks and an overgrown field
next to an abandoned warehouse on the other side of rue Notre-
Dame, you can find a place to watch the night work of the Port
of Montreal. The cranes come alive, moving containers on and
off ships, onto railcars and tractor trailers. Halogens like pulsars,
giving daylight. If you look hard, you can see the men inside the
cranes, pulling the levers. seamless, this work is, and its rhythms.
There are too many feral cats around for us to worry about rats.
broken glass lying in wait under grass is really the only threat.
you just need to brush your hand lightly over the blades before
you sit down.
        The cranes are so large, hulking gray and orange,
not flamingos or giraffes but anteaters with long hungry
snouts. they seem nearby. they are not.                they
are huge and distant. and apart from the occasional squeal
of a turbine or the thud of a large container being stacked
and loaded, the whole sympathy is silent.        so, we can sit.
still.    and talk or think or whatever.



Night.

Ely is trying to have a conversation with Marie-Ève. She refuses to close the car door or take the key out of the ignition. *Ding. Ding. Ding. Ding.* keeping time as he speaks. The interior light is on, the passenger side filled with fast food containers and a purse spilling its contents over the seat and into the footwell.

*Ding. Ding. Ding. Ding.*

"No, no, that's not what happened. . . . No, you need to talk with him. . . . *calice*, I can't call him. . . . *puis-je* . . . I can't." Who the fuck knows where she's going. How does she even have money for gas? Ely asks not wanting to know the answer.

"*Elle*————*un cauchemar.*" she—this—is a nightmare.

Marie-Ève has dyed her hair deep red on top of a recent bleaching.          braided frizzy pigtails.          during the moments away from him, a world          of re-fashioned living.          entirely of her own making.          he knows that. But when their friend died, it was Ely who felt responsible to be there for Marie-Ève.     friends.     he took her pain.     no blame. in fact, no questions. he accepted what she gave. and that was a little less than a year ago. There was even a short period of time, between this time and now, when Marie-Ève more-or-less disappeared          too

          not-dead-but-there          more-or-less disappeared from his life.

she was somewhere, yes. thank god. but not here. with him. he just
never wants her to be no-where.

it's hard for him to be there for a friend whose loss he feels is so
near, so on-the-verge-of-loss, after another friend's death.

she is her, separated by a year.
two small deaths.

just one not yet.

*"ne sait-elle pas?"*     she has to

it is hard to relax, not to feel on the edge.
to feel the edge. he waits.

musical chairs, substitution, repetition, anticipation.
pre-mourning (God what a thought). Everyone is living

pre- and post-

III.

# A HUNDRED TIMES

here goes.

I.

*Cent fois*, at least that many, measured against
the final one.

2.

They decide to clean up her room,     in the end.         like
the decision had been predetermined.         the task was
simply waiting for them to find awareness.
                                                    in the end.
What was the significance of Catherine's things? there was
nothing to suggest that these objects held any importance to
her.         other than the fact that they were in fact
hers.       nothing told them that one object had more to say about
her than any other. did her jewelry box or alarm clock capture
more of
her     her-ness?
or was it the collection of metallic beads hanging from the
bedpost or the wastepaper basket that screamed,

"It's me! Catherine!"?

they were asking a lot of this messy room.

her mother felt morbid telling her sister that she pulled all the
hairs from Catherine's brush, collecting them in an envelope.
tucked in her underwear drawer. The envelope joined a sachet
of baby teeth and a small piece of dried umbilicus. She also took
Catherine's lip gloss. She planned to someday open it and touch it
to her own lips.   when she needed it.                    later.
for now,
                                                 time to clean
                                                    the room.

3.

It was probably Catherine who made the stains on the
living room carpet.

they've hung around longer        than her.

which is a shitty thing to say.
a shitty thing to know.

4.

the medicine cabinet is rid of his things but where his razor once
was, permanent black stubble fills the seam between the shelf and
the mirror. can she ever escape these material entanglements? the
aggressive stuff-ness of absence?

5.

He owed so many people money.     so. many.

                                  people come looking.

It is not hard to figure out who-belongs-to-who

                                  when something is
owed.

6.

Ely left the grief support group complaining that no one
wants to talk about bodies.   real bodies. sure they care
about ways to hold onto memory : not deleting voicemails :
taking care to save photos in the cloud.
they talk about missing what a person did or didn't do :
missing their warmth in bed or their laughter.
but without bodies, none of these things matter.


           "    *faker,*    "            he says.


he wonders aloud,         how can you talk about missing the
sound of his voice if you're unwilling to talk about missing
the shape of his cock?

7.

What is rescue distance if not a fire station next to
Dèzèry Square?

the city or neighbors or some of the local business owners put a
porta potty in the park.

Old men and women shuffle between benches and picnic tables.
Everyone is up to something. But it's more like a waiting room
than a park. The firefighters are smoking and laughing in front of
the large garage doors of the station.
un-idle, still
everyone is waiting.

8.

some. time. maybe in the next 1000 years / of human
history / our moment will be remembered as the time of
the insects.              greedy for crumbs, the blind
labor of accumulation that comes at the expense of
everything else.              this is what self-sabotage
looks like.       unkind unthinkingly.         we traded a
Greek chorus for outreach vans and prevention slogans.
boy-oh-boy-oh-boy


there will be books written about us.                  we will
end in a punch line.           scholars will present our lack
of regard and failed compassion as evidence of our
          lapsed humanity.         our membership in the human tribe
will be put on notice.
our expulsion all but assured.

good riddance.
in retrospect.

it's only noon.

9.

He is here once again in their company.      this is what is called
support.          also, a space for joy or rawness or silences.
it calls on him to trust even after the world has betrayed his.

he can't always give.
but he's here.

10.

"How far back do you want me to go?"

11.

He was fine until he heard the first-floor neighbors
laughing. Never mind what.
So many things can set him off.

His mood has to be just-so to avoid what comes next.

no, not avoid, to be anything else besides, his factory
setting.

12.

We completed one loop, giving our first names.
The psychiatrist who corrected the counselor to use Dr.
begins his
mini lecture on the grief cycle. he asks if anyone has heard
of Kübler-Ross without waiting for a response.
"I know it's tough, I know it's tough" finds its way into the
moments between each thought.
it works as a vacant form of conjugation.

his "ummmmm."

it telegraphs that another bit of wisdom is coming.

so don't interrupt.

a grief group of nine polite, hurting people,

and one magnificent jackass.

13.

Write a letter to your future self, he suggests.

14.

"Do you remember a time from your childhood when you felt helpless?"

my lord. where is this heading?

15.

tone, shift.    yes, someone uses drugs, still, even in her
after. they say it out loud.
this-now-exposed-druggie-pariah has just broken the fourth wall
of grief support. we enter the icky real.
the psychiatrist scrambles to keep the actors on stage.


Dr. is forced to allow subtext to pass into text.
drugs : bad
he suddenly not surprisingly gains one or two allies.


grief support. a world where no sea between exists.
only one landmass at odds with another.        pushing.
plate tectonics.    friction.    good vs. bad (evil?)
bellowed clichés.


no two things can be true at once.        to use and to feel.
and suddenly one person's hurt doesn't count as much.


What on earth are we doing here?    How did it come to this?

16.

                                        The workshop is
about to begin.
at the outset we are told there is no such thing as an
accidental overdose. not really.


The first presenter begins by outlining the primary causes of
accidental overdose and their prevention.

17.

He leaves the meeting dampened.     worn out.
facts. do nothing for his loss.

18.

support.
support groups.
support as hearing and talking. a fresh supply each time.
he talks about what kind of support he could have used before
his loss. he speculates. there's really nothing that could have been
done.
for him.
he was just bracing for impact.
now sorting through the wreckage.

19.

His thoughts are homeless in these meetings.

and plentiful.

20.

Marie-Ève leaves the apartment smelling like an ashtray.
      He loved her.
that smell, the smell of love is the smell of.

of rubbing alcohol and body odor.

21.

god, what I wouldn't give for a little myth. one or two
woodland sprites and some natural magic.
amid all this bluntness.

22.

I have written the phrase "the work of mourning" so many times
in my fieldnotes.
it's not so much a          note-to-self : it's a header.
I describe these conversations and the things they reveal as
the work of mourning. I don't know why everything seems to
conform to this rubric so neatly.
Shouldn't it?                 note-to-self : find new subheadings soon.

23.

This is. not just.
Not just the work of not-vanishing. not just the work of
working against vanishing on behalf of the vanished.
not just.

24.

and if it's love's work. not just. then too is it the work of a belly
full. of sick.        about to be released.

25.

I ask, "What questions should I be asking? What should I ask if I want to know something about grief, about the experience of losing someone to overdose?"

26.

He asks, "What do you think you mean when you say
overdose? or loss?"

                    not just.          but loss all the same.

27.

overdose and its metaphors.

good lord.

28.

I ask, "What's the one thing you want to remember about your time with her?"

Ely asks, "Only one?"

Now my turn for stupid questions.

29.

She was run over by a car.  She stumbled out into traffic high as
fuck.                    *are you fucking serious?*
Is that overdose?        Does it count?
Who keeps score?         and why?

30.

It begins like all love stories, in line at a soup kitchen.
he was waiting at the entrance of the Église Notre-Dame-
de-la-Salette.
she had been volunteering for several months by then.

31.

He was a lost cause     but cute.

32.

They were given three glorious months.
"We were given . . ."
She continues to volunteer.

33.

Catherine did not bathe    often.    It was common
knowledge among her roommates. It was a source of
pride for her.          her olfactory protest.

34.

I suppose in the end there are traces, in one form or another.
I suppose it's good to leave an impression. odor from beyond.

35.

Ely's former landlord insisted that Marie-Ève pay his rent
for the last four months of his lease. it was totally illegal,
also unfair and petty. she couldn't. so, he held onto his
things.

there wasn't much, mostly junk, but still. and the guy
probably just dumped it all.     in the end.

36.

to add insult to injury. the telephone company wanted her
to pay a cancellation fee for his phone and cable service.
they shared an account.    credit ratings in the age of
overdose death.
an economic study yet to be made.

      but apparently needed.

37.

"   I said he was poisoned.    I say he was murdered.   "

38.

the relationship between intrigue and empathy is easy and
icky.

but useful.

39.

He died of alcohol. This is how he describes his brother's
death. no one questions it. at least not openly.
"Is this the overdose we're talking about?"
                                the question registers on a
                                few faces.

40.

retro deaths. & old epidemics.

which crisis are we talking about now?    of now?    exactly?

COVID has all but vanished from our discussions.

41.

you have entered the waiting room.
waiting for the organizer to start the meeting.
the moments before the Zoom call are so much worse than the
meetings themselves.
when we are let in, we welcome the social pressure. to stay.
once your face appears.
on the screen. with others.

having no exit feels safe.
but these few minutes of waiting are brutal.

42.

faced with the possibility of escape or avoidance. it is just
     too much today. leave meeting.

43.

all she wants to remember is Ely catching snow on his
tongue. and laughing.

together.

44.

she is replacing everything else with this. this image.     she
does not want to hear that she has things she needs to work
through. grief's work.
it is all tongue and snow now.

45.

I recommend the French translation of Max Porter's *Grief
Is the Thing with Feathers* to Catherine. I end up gifting her
a copy. the line between the seminar room and field is
getting blurrier.              I rejoice. in the growing meta.

46.

Who really wants to receive these stories    really?    these.
every.    tedious attempts to remember or forget or rewrite
or restore?    Every discussion is making the problem of
reception clearer.

everyone wants to hear.
no one wants to hear.

both impulses feel wrong and justified.

47.

She reminds the group, "your common experience doesn't mean common ground."

I like this.
we nod. each box in the Zoom gallery. a collection of bobbleheads.

48.

"I can't imagine."
a phrase that suddenly means something.

49.

We are now discussing what's required to receive another's
story.
No one has been asked to share anything.

not yet.

I like this moderator.
a lot.

50.

They become dust.    we breathe them in.
they mix. grit and spit.
joined with our tears and saliva.

51.

Someone asks, "why?" "   why?    " is it chance, bad luck,
fate?      no one chimes in.      the same old question
recycled.

There is no equation to balance. no theorem to prove.
The search for reason. a reason for seeking reasons.

pish posh.
jellybeans and navel lint make about as much sense.

52.

I like this moderator.

a lot.

53.

they are still here.

remainders.

And you. living beyond them.

54.

Someone mentions opioids.

55.

Buckle up.

56.

we form a queue.
to give two cents.
maybe three.
this loss creates experts.    who never asked for it.

57.

There are few topics that give each group member a chance
to share their own sociological thesis so candidly.
not *so* but *too*.
few topics blur fact and conjecture so aggressively.
few push people to political poles so dramatically.
clumsily.
underlying causes, debates about responsibility, Purdue
Pharma's avoidance of that responsibility, Sackler family
wealth and legacy, hydrocodone, hydromorphone,
oxycodone, fentanyl, codeine, prescribing practices of bad
doctors and dentists, pain, pain's denial, need, want, the
war on drugs.

victims, dealers, enablers, bad families, good families, that
one guy who, choice, systems failures, and personal
failures.

our blood pressures have risen. it is time to take a break.

58.

continuous opioid overdose death crisis.
rolls off the tongue.

59.

Marie-Ève says she doesn't feel there's enough time.
others agree. there are two clocks. ticking.
the first is the one that's increasingly slowed by the desire to
understand, to feel, to move within a loss. whatever its time,
whatever time it needs, you need, is the correct time. She reminds
herself of this fact.
the second is the clock watched by others. impatient. for her to get
over it. to come back from wherever his loss has placed her.
time and travel distance. it is like others think she's taking
something from them by taking her own time. a finite resource. it
puts something about shared time in jeopardy.

60.

*ahem*, moving on.

61.

Everyone on the Zoom call can hear her kids playing and fighting in the background.

It is hard to tell if she notices.

62.

How to keep things tidy?      Do you call a babysitter to
make time to talk about a dead brother? Is it the same time
as the rest of your time or is this some other time that needs
to be made? manifested?

63.

What bullshit is this? to take time out for the thing that has
already pushed its way into the center of your every day.
all of them.

64.

He died and left the stove on and the front door open.

65.

surprise, surprise. she says.    Funerals are expensive.

66.

She wanted to read the eulogy she had written to the group.

but she lost her nerve.

67.

What is more heartbreaking than someone hurting,
fumbling to find the right words? There are so many
scripts floating around,
scripts for telling-one's-process-of-bereavement,
empty and ready-made, so that the slightest falter in the
search to put word and feeling together looks like

     pure

                 lunacy.

**68.**

stick to the script.

69.

duh. *non deuil.*

70.

more love for the despised. She has had it with
goody-goodies. everyone loved Ely before. now,
not so much. he's keeping bad company in death.

71.

Dream time. again.   He returns incompletely.   He doesn't
ask for anything, but she senses a want. his. all the same.

She has nothing to give.

can't give.

72.

brutal, this blame, asleep or awake.

73.

her lies. and his.

74.

He left to visit family in Haïti.

He returned to a dead sister.

75.

She believes in reincarnation but doesn't want to speculate about          this life.

76.

the logics of punishment and salvation
should stay out of it.

77.

work.    hang at the park.    work.    hang at the park.

nothing has changed.

78.

there are so many.

gone.

79.

Everyone here has a hole.

80.

She carries Naloxone now.    Nicorette and Naloxone.
her new little    habits.

81.

They were going to take his ashes to Île-Bonaventure-et-du-Rocher-Percé, to spread them at the end of the Gaspé Peninsula, where the land meets the sea.

 she is waiting on friends to find time.

 everyone works.

 the trip loses its poetry

 to scheduling.

82.

His text messages are pushed further down the list. toward
a cliff.

83.

She let her five-year-old niece fall into an open
construction pit.        they didn't ask if she was stoned,
they knew
*être camé* walking their girl home from school.
months of recovery.
they will never. forgive her. after that. not even now.
after her.


a fairy tale. a child thrown down a well. a witch, to blame.

84.

every story, the eager assignment of guilt and guiltlessness.

85.

She sounds suddenly fiercely Christian.　　　　　　but not
one of the good ones.

86.

She is done listening.

87.

She doesn't use the bus stop where they found him.
Landscapes of avoidance

                    that no one gives a
       shit about.

88.

the guy at the picnic table is nodding off.      for now
ignored,          until he turns blue.

89.

all this repeats.

90.

a hundred times he acted like a cringey asshole.

91.

a hundred times she slipped from his thoughts.

92.

a hundred times running into his friends.

93.

a hundred dollars spent on nothing.

94.

it happened a hundred times. to all of them.

95.

a hundred "I wish he was heres."

96.

a hundred photos deleted from her phone          and recovered.
only to be deleted again.

97.

a hundred times without.

98.

a hundred of the same.    and more.

99.

a hundred times.

100.

we all know what happens next.

# IV. THIS IS WHAT YOU DESERVE

The kitchen was hot pink. The cabinets were white with hot pink accents; hot pink carefully painted by Marie-Ève along the thin trim that framed each door. The living room was yellow and white.    Some of the outlet covers were hot pink, until the paint ran out. others were white.

Her eyes were blue.

When they moved into the apartment it was the first improvement Ely and Marie-Ève made. brightening. It was obvious. the colors were Marie-Ève's favorites. They matched her uniform: head-to-toe camouflage, her pants a mix of standard greens, but her top, a blend of camo greens and pink, pink shoes, and a large yellow fanny pack. The color of the kitchen was less washed out, more electric than her outfit and the thousands of pink objects she owned. she owned, they loved. the yellow was her yellow to the letter.

    The landlord said it was okay if they promised to paint it white when they moved out.

The trees outside the dining room window are completely
still. The room is quiet and gray, a darker echo of the trees.
a before stillness. She bought plants that seem to be doing
well. benign neglect. the secret to her green thumb. the
sun muted, flat, holds everything in place. Just enough
light for faint shadows to form on the floor along the
bookshelves. but still. an empty room.
or unoccupied.
what's the difference? without a homecoming.

Thunderheads appear in the early evening. each orange and
blue sucking white energy to its center. The horizon is so
dark    the base of the clouds makes it look like a mountain
range has spontaneously burst from the flatlands.
cotton monstrosities making a new terrain.

The small, bright dining room and its neighbor, hot pink
and glowing, brace for the storm. not hail but such large
droplets of rain they rap hard on the glass, sometimes like
bursts of sand thrown against the pane. The windows are
old over-painted and gaped. water enters along odd seams
in little pools tracking dirt dust and dead leaves trapped in
the windowsill at the end of last summer. the slow even
sound of dripping is coming from somewhere inside the
apartment, which is super unnerving. but also freeing.
since no one is here to notice.

or drown.

It's the made bed not the crumpled sheets that is absence.

It's the empty kitchen sink and the undisturbed pillows.

It is everything exactly where you left it.

It is tidiness that shows ache.

Just keep going.

The storm ends by morning. The photos hanging on the wall, or rather the figures in those photos, watch. These things that lingered around them never once announce themselves. It is wrong to say these objects (photos, keepsakes) have gone quiet. They always needed warm bodies to complete the circuit. They needed the contact of people to become animated. waiting, patiently, between sun and storm, lovingly, or like a tick, perched on a leaf or a branch. waiting to drop down on someone unsuspecting, to find a bloodmeal. waiting.

this waiting they do, these ticks, unable to fly so they settle for persistence and falling—the term for this lazy necessary technique is *questing*. Ely and Marie-Ève's objects were questing, waiting to descend on who comes along, after.

At what point is it appropriate to edit the environment? to turn the place of *we* into *I* ?          the frenzied quest to rearrange the furniture,

                              someone once wrote.

Ely woke up. Marie-Ève did not. Neither returns.


Her sick was puce, not pink, deader than that color they

shared.

There is no border between horror and melancholy.

Or maybe there is, elsewhere.

But not here.

No secret passage revealed by experience.
No line.
Not any amount of what is felt gives advantage.
Not stretched or condensed by time. or by or with others.

Here are wants. And asking about them only makes them
wilder by exposure.

Paint peels in the sun or is scratched away madly by
bloodied broken nails.

The result is the same.

Scream this fact.

# nothing.
## is what you
## expect.

fingers
slammed in a
kitchen
drawer.

*Go ahead.* rewind, just a little.

The feeling starts in his throat.   it squeezes.

disbelief moves to the front of Ely's mind.

weighty, a tingle, a shudder.

thick. He waits and it passes.

Gone.

She is gone.


Ely drives, his mind unfolds, a wave builds again. The car radio does nothing to drown out his thoughts. She is gone, and now a little panic.

orange and blue

is a pricking awareness that something vital has been neglected, but what? an unattended flame. it's in a space of half-formed thoughts where his dread trespasses. inert and potent.

and then the swell releases and leaves him with a calm that only ever required him to acknowledge that it is all his fault. simple.

quiet and total

that the wrongs he owns have eaten whatever sense of good
he might have once felt about himself. digested, pulse
slows to acceptance.

he pulls a blanket over his thoughts,          of her, them
          and tucks himself into this vacant feeling as car
headlights stream past him and


dusk arrives.    again.

*There was a before.*

The party he threw for her the year before she died,   she
never considered birthdays very special,      but she danced
and smiled until her face hurt.

friends filled the room. they made her a cake, vanilla with
chocolate frosting and pink and yellow sprinkles. there was
beer and champagne. She wore a green vintage dress,
sleeveless, with flowers, low-cut in the back and tight
around her waist.

and danced.


did they even speak that night?      a halo of light

surrounded her.

No one could make a night so un-silent or sing so lovingly.

he just watched her.

so many times,                    so easy now to recall,
     when he wishes that he'd been alert to the

importance of being.  there.    with her.




but this was one.        he knew it then.



he just watched her.    in a room of laughter
their yellow turned turmeric gold ringed in pearl, as flash
disappears into night.

Together.

Ely and Marie-Ève.

blameless enraged and never whole again.
        love, burning pink and yellow.
Rewind, *just a little*, to that point and start the tape again.
Life deserves a little editing now and then.
love, passing slowly, nicotine yellow reflections of a setting
sun against the bookcase, through a window from which
they both took warmth.

one wish dropped in buckets.

a want.                                terrible, this

want, and fierce.

in the end.    a soft place to land

is what you deserve.

a chance for something more,                   after

her end.

# be still.

close your eyes.

make a wish.

ACKNOWLEDGMENTS

I am grateful to the people who spoke with me about friends, lovers, and family, and about their lives in and around loss. I wrote a book about grief, but that is not the same as understanding it. I pulled thin filaments from the dense and tangled weave of living and then stretched and twisted those strands, reshaping them. Stories, observations, hints, and invitations that often felt like intrusions became method. Marie-Ève, Catherine, and Ely—all and each of them— are pseudonyms. I appreciate the encouragement of Jenn Ashworth, Richard Baxstrom, Sam Byers, Nancy Campbell, Robert Desjarlais, Coline Fournout, Fanny Gutiérrez-Meyers, Hannah Landecker, Chris Kelty, Ramzi Nimr, Eugene Raikhel, Pamela Reynolds, Andrés Romero, and Anthony Stavrianakis. The book is dedicated to Stefanos Geroulanos for all the reasons. Ken Wissoker and the creative minds at Duke University Press are remarkable. Finally, I am grateful for ongoing support through the endowed professorship created by the Marjorie and Gerald Bronfman Foundation in the Department of Social Studies of Medicine at McGill University.